T0130505

ANOTHER HORIZON

MARSHA E. BEIGHLEY

iUniverse, Inc.
Bloomington

Another Horizon

Copyright © 2011 Marsha E. Beighley

All rights reserved. No part of this book may be used or reproduced by
any means, graphic, electronic, or mechanical, including photocopying,
recording, taping or by any information storage retrieval system
without the written permission of the publisher except in the case
of brief quotations embodied in critical articles and reviews.

iUniverse books may be ordered through booksellers or by contacting:

iUniverse
1663 Liberty Drive
Bloomington, IN 47403
www.iuniverse.com
1-800-Authors (1-800-288-4677)

Because of the dynamic nature of the Internet, any Web addresses or
links contained in this book may have changed since publication and
may no longer be valid. The views expressed in this work are solely those
of the author and do not necessarily reflect the views of the publisher,
and the publisher hereby disclaims any responsibility for them.

Any people depicted in stock imagery provided by Thinkstock are models,
and such images are being used for illustrative purposes only.

Certain stock imagery © Thinkstock.

ISBN: 978-1-4620-0059-3 (pbk)
ISBN: 978-1-4620-0060-9 (ebk)

Printed in the United States of America

iUniverse rev. date: 3/10/2011

This book is for the two best people
in my life, Earl and Mom.

Contents

Unicorns

In a quiet, green glade, a unicorn once lay,
Amid wild flowers in bloom, no shadow or gloom.
The sun shone brightly on snowy white,
with ivory hoof and horn.
He is but one unicorn.
There is a slight tramp of feet, into the
glade many more of them meet.
Unicorns many from the world abroad, some ugly,
some pure beauty, and one odd,
from Japan, with a horn or two,
The Ki'lin and their cousin the Kirin.
The heavy, huge warrior Kakardan
and a ghostly herald of death for man.
One like a black ass with a horn of blood,
and a little web-toed creature colored like mud.
Each one a unicorn, each possessing power in one horn.
He joins them as a brother, his white form but only another.
Each a powerful spirit to man,
Unicorns each as unique as thoughts can be.
Pureness of body, in a scientific lobby;
Peace in a unicorn, or war in one horn.
In a quiet glade, a unicorn once lay.
He is but one in mind;
A unicorn for anyone you will find.

A Humble Hero

Once upon a time,
There was a story given no rhyme.
The humblest hero,
His name had no sir; it was just plain Leero.

He had no proud steed,
Only a mule and one fantastic deed.
You see, there was a horrific dragon,
Bigger than the largest wagon.

The dragon kidnapped the governor's daughter.
This flustered the governor, so he wouldn't eat or drink water.
This dragon made a pet of the maid,
And enjoyed his every village raid.

This was until he met Leero,
And the way that man became a hero.
He stole into the dragon's lair.
While the beast slept, he freed the maiden fair.

He paused just at the cave mouth outside;
On the mule the maid went, quickly did she ride.
He climbed above the cave;
A good shove to a rock he gave.

Down came many rocks in a crash.
This sealed in the dragon with his latest stash.
For days the dragon was trapped in,
Alone in the darkness of his den.

Then the day came,
Leero made the dragon look weak, even lame.
The dragon soon begged;
Too cruel was this deed to man or four legged.

Leero and the dragon made to agree
That the dragon wouldn't harm anything he could see.
The dragon crept out, nothing but skin and bone.
He fled to the mountains and was gone.

Then Leero refused to be labeled a hero,
No sir or knight, just plain Leero.
His only gain from his deed,
A wife of the maid and a better steed.
He lived happily ever after,
His home full of children and laughter.

The end.

Quick Silver

Quick Silver body of black.
Quick Silver hair of sterling.
Quick Silver horn of sapphire.
Quick Silver great charger.
Quick Silver stride knight less.
Quick Silver honor of beauty.
Quick Silver king of love.
Quick Silver pure of heart.

Celestial Dragon

Red, lacquered scales shining.
Black eyes gleam knowledge.
Dagger talons.
White sphere of knowledge.
Wise gaze upon smooth white.

Perfect Creatures

These perfect creatures:
The ki'lin,
As dainty as calves.
As fierce as lions,
Adorned with colored scales.

Cats and Things

Kittens and strings,
Cats and things.
This is what cats play with.
A kitten and a tree that's too tall,
A cat and a brightly colored ball.
This is what cats play with.
A kitten and mouse tails,
A cat and balancing on fence rails.
This is what cats play with.
A kitten and a furry fluff,
A cat and mommy's makeup puff.
This is what cats play with.
A kitten and a scuttling bug,
A cat and poking around in a coffee mug.
This is what cats play with.
And best of all,
Strings and things.
This is what cats play with.

Another Mile

The air was crisp and cold,
the road unused and old.
I walked with slow footfall,
when I heard a lone crow call.
The road came upon a brook,
overgrown with cattails in every nook.
The bold maple with fiery leaves,
the color of an old barn's eaves.
Maple amidst old burly pine,
and for a moment, I thought it all mine.
I crossed the bridge to the other side,
from me a quail flew to hide.
Then my lips parted to smile;
maybe I'd walk another mile.
The air gained a subtle heat,
like hot pies we like to eat.
I froze in place and cocked my head,
but my senses all seemed dead.
Cinnamon filled the air
on the breeze that mussed my hair.
Suddenly, I thought I saw a unicorn,
his purity of coat and ivory horn.
But when I turned to see,
the view did escape me.
Maybe all I had seen was in mind,
and there was nothing behind.
If only the oak could talk;
Another mile I think I'll walk.

Cherry Blossoms

Delicate, light blooms,
Sweet, pink blooms
Falling quietly down.
Falling toward a
Smooth mirror of glass.

Drops Wet Fall

Drops wet fall,
Puddles gather full.
A stream babbling runs,
River dragons play,
Rivers flow wide.
The gulf harbors boats,
Hippocampus sleeps silent.
The sea rocks a boat,
Beneath mermaids dance.
Above clouds gather,
Clouds grow dark.
Drops wet fall.

Lighter Pleasures

Many are ours, the lighter pleasures.
We take of them.
We take them for granted.
A warm smile or thank you.
A cold sip of water,
A slice of bread with meat,
Take time to take of lighter pleasures.
Another day to do with as you wish,
A glance of a sunset afire with color,
A bloom brightly open.
Many forms are lighter pleasures.
Some for one, some for others.
A child's laugh, a lost penny found,
A kitten's soft rub, a friend's warm hug.
Daily are our lighter pleasures.
Count them and wonder in their abundance.
A crisp, sweet apple,
Shady trees to sit under, a favorite book,
That old comfortable shirt.
Take of your daily pleasure.
Live life fully, for it brims with pleasure.

Contentment

I know not this feeling,
which flows over me like a tide.
I do not know if it is sorrow,
or is it happiness?
I do know it moves me,
but where or why?
It alighted upon my heart,
from where I am not certain.
I savor this feeling for, like the harder earned love never lasts.
Contentment,
like in itself, the love of a moment, but as ever, a moment never lasts.

A Fantasy Stew

Here is how to make fantasy stew.
You need a pot for it to brew.
First, you need fairy dance on dew.
Then add a knight or two.
Don't forget the princess all new.
Remember the dragons and trolls but only a few.
Most important is imagining from you.
Don't forget your dreams, too.

Horses

Rolling thunder across a plain.
Moving bodies of powerful grace.
Each makes to take the lead.
Faster. Faster they race past.

A Dove. A Gate.

Love is soft as a dove.
Hate is as harsh as a locked gate.
A gate goes nowhere.
A dove can fly beyond.

Kaleidoscope Cover

Patches of color.
Red, blue, and green.
Carefully sewn.
Lovingly placed and matched.
Mixed to delight me.
I snuggle under loving warmth.

Dragonfly

Crystal-winged, tiny, little dragon,
He gently skims the pond's glassy surface,
Dancing with a mirrored partner.
Thunder announces the coming of a spring shower,
He darts amid reed and grass,
Perching finally upon cattail fluff to brave the coming rain.

Fairy Dance

Deep in forest glade,
Where fairy rings are made,
Is a place where you may see
Fairies playing flutes on high key.

At first things are slow,
But soon pick up and are on the go.
They with shiny wings dance,
And with wildness they prance.

They go 'round and 'round,
And make a ring on the ground,
That tomorrow will grow mushrooms,
In the grass for making brooms.

If Life Was Simple...

If life was simple for dragons,
Knights would come with can openers.
So be thankful life isn't simple…

Tiger

Tiger's soft fleet feet.
Lightly moving shadows.
Gold and black amid thick green.
Dancing with shy prey.

Philosophic

People say I'm too philosophic,
Because I think and talk on any subject.

Good versus Evil

The old courtyard is empty, silent,
And no people celebrate their king's reign.
The old stone gargoyles are silent;
They watch the sun and rain.

The yard is overgrown, the roses shapeless briars,
Not very separate from the woods.
No people live here; they no longer burn fires;
The cobweb strewn walls are in eerie moods.

He is here, violent and old.
His blood and breath are burning evil.
From the people he took the king's gold.
He is a creature medieval.

He is a dragon.
Pure incarnate of greed,
He stood strong against a wizard's flagon.
He defeated many knights with blinding speed.

His foe,
He is just as old.
He is soft, mellow as a doe.
His heart is not for gold.

The castle is old, unused.
He could smell the evil.
He was angry, not amused,
For he knew this creature medieval.

He ventured into the courtyard.
He found no people good or other,
Or the princess he loved and her kingly father.

He is a unicorn,
A creature of love and pureness.
Healing and good come of his horn,
With this he turns away evil with sureness.

So to battle they both face,
Both stood their ground.
One did so with grace;
One did with the pouncing crouch like a hound.

He wanted the castle for good;
He wanted the castle, too, but for evil.
The unicorn's power hung over him like a hood,
But the dragon's greed held firmly vile.

He, the unicorn, sighed looking down upon him,
For he wasn't afraid.
The dragon's chance grew dim;
He'd lose without aide.

Unicorn, he is king,
To good the dragon bows.
For in him greed was dying,
He'd leave this castle forever, he vows.

Robot

I speak as you. I see as you.
I hear as you. I bleed as you.
I have flesh and bone as you.
You see me a robot, as inhuman.
I work for need.
You do not need to work, being without need.
You are god? I am a robot?
Do you think I am a servant of you?
You are powerful. I am not.
Why am I a machine for you?
You look down upon me.
You put your car above me.
I must work. You don't have to.
I must sweat. You do nothing.
You think you are the master.
I am your machine.
I serve you so I may eat.
You eat my pride because I serve you.

I am a robot.

You live in a home. I have a closet.
Money makes some god?
In the end I get peace.
It is you who gets to be plugged in.

Serpent Horse

Serpent horse, you sly hippocampus,
You're so menacing; you do frighten us.
You are part snake, and you are part horse;
You belong in tales of ancient Norse.
But unlike the tales of long ago,
You refuse to vanish, and you refuse to go.
You live in the sea;
Hidden away in shadow you'll forever be.
Although you hide from our sight,
You amaze us with your beauty and might.
Today you don't tackle boats.
You, hippocampus, are not the size of billy goats.
You are quite alive and you still live,
To children joy you give.
In fact you are not all that mighty,
You are indeed quite tiny.
Hippocampus is your science name,
But you are a sea horse to the scientifically maim.

My Book

I finish reading you,
So I return you to your shelven nook.
You sit side by side,
With books for poetry, science, and how to cook.
But you are different;
You are special, because you are my book.
I read you from cover to cover, even gave you a second look.
Now you are back in the library.
But once I had to choose, it was you I took.
I may return again,
Take you home again or another book.
I will remember,
If I feel sad or lonely or bored, I know where to look.

Captured Hearts

She sat in a somber mood,
Her soft form all nude.
In the garden sitting, willing to wait,
She gazed upon the open garden gate.

She knew he would come,
There was nothing that could be done.
In through the gate he strode,
Pure grace and power in his mode.

He knelt, soft nose to her breast.
He lies down; in her lap his head will rest.
She caresses his velvet alabaster skin,
For him his heart she did win.

Come the ones who sought the unicorn,
But all they want is his life saving horn.
A cold spear did bring him death,
Stopping forever his sweet breath.

The men took away their prize.
She didn't follow; she made no effort to rise.
His death gripped her heart with grief,
From this pain there was no relief.

Until the day of her last breath,
She would remember the unicorn's death.

Hearts

Hearts symbolize love.
Hearts playing cards.
Hearts portraying joy.
Heart-shaped candies.
Hearts for a little happiness.
Hearts meaning unity.
Hearts just for fun.
Hearts on valentine cards.
Hearts of childhood memories.

Bubbles

Clear, iridescent spheres,
More delicate than glass,
As light as air,
Burst upon spring grass.

Unicorn

Soft, little unicorn,
With one silver horn.
Light pink of a wild rose,
Blushes your soft nose.
Purest blue of a cloudless sky,
Does reflect the color of your eye.
Your coat is purest white;
It sparkles like snow in pale winter light.

Time

Time does build up mountains,
Then bury them in the sea.
Time lets nations rise,
Then later they no longer be.

Time has seen dinosaurs huge,
And has harbored a simple flea.
Time has seen grasses many,
And the sprouting of every ageless tree.

Time has seen many things,
And from it we may not flee.
Time lets things live,
It lets things die,
But time will forever be.

Lion

Power and grace beckon for
A kingly beast crowned.
Round eyes gaze sternly upon
A scorched dry kingdom.
All of Africa his queen.

Another Shade of Purple

What is blue?
A pond or the sky?
There is more to blue.
The sky is blue up high;
Underneath it is more.
As the pond ripples,
It reflects the sky with the touch of an oar.
The blue deepens with the day's end.
So the sky changes color,
And the pond did the same.
What is blue but another shade of purple?

Journeyman

He is a journeyman;
With him he takes a cup and pan.
He fixes food in his pan,
And sleeps where he can.

He travels from coast to coast,
And drinks his ale always with a toast.
His favorite food is beef roast,
And he can eat the most.

He is a journeyman,
And he has a dark tan.
His name is Zeppernan;
With him he carries a cup and pan.

Moon

Nighttime watcher,
On a cold blanket of stars.
A cold, ever-changing face,
Moods upon a disk of faded color.

In My Hands

Here I stand,
Book in hand.
I hold it,
Open a bit.
Someone read,
For knowledge I need.
For sadly,
I read badly.
So teach me.
To read would set me free.

Magic

Magic is power.
Magic is good.
Magic is evil.
Magic is everywhere.
Magic is nowhere.
Magic is love.
Magic is hate.
Magic is a cure.
Magic is the ill.
Magic is new.
Magic is old.
Magic is in the Earth.
Magic is in the Sky.
Magic is human.
Magic is alien.
Magic is anything.
Magic is everything.
Magic is the power of dreams.

Back around Again

It must come back around.
Begin it must in the ground.
Seed feed on soil then sprout and grow.
All types of it, more than grass abound.

Gazelle and zebra feast upon new green growth.
They must feed on it, and they become round.
Lion spot such a bounty of flesh.
To sustain it they consume meat to the last pound.

The predator must give it away with the last gasp of breath.
Flesh must return to the ground.
It must come back around again.

Tumbleweed Land

Open stretches of sun-baked sand
Are a no-man's-land.
A land of outlaws and cattle,
And where tough men live in a saddle.
A place by which a gun may rule,
And small towns see outlaws duel.
This is the Wild West,
A place to test even the hardiest.
Nothing but coyotes, cactus, and sand, this is tumbleweed land.

Peacock

A proud, handsome prince is
dressed in an eye-plumed cloak.
Impressing the ladies
with iridescent blues and green.
Adore the crown prince.
The most royal of fowl, the peacock.

A Self-Portrait

A self-portrait is a mere photo of me,
Done by me.
A self-portrait is merely a reflection of me,
A face I see in the mirror.
A self-portrait, unlike a photo or reflection,
With care is rendered, taking a part of me.

Last Dawn

Dawn streams through
A forest of tangled bamboo.
Warm light falls upon a sleeper,
Alighting a body colored like molten fire.
Stirring from slumber,
The sleeper wakes.
Alighting to his feet,
He silently strides into the thicket.
Pausing, his golden eyes peer upward,
One last look into his world.
His tail flicks sharply once,
Then he trots away.
The bamboo jungle swallows the last Bali,
Our last red tiger.

Sea Sprites

Happy sprites of the sea,
Smooth, silvery creatures
With laughing faces.
They have the blue deep;
Their playground oceans be.
Playing in the wake of boats,
Racing the waves,
Then onward for a leaping spree.
They live a life of diving,
In deep seas forever swimming.
Each is as busy as a happy bee.
They're content as peas in a pod,
Dolphin families in the oceans,
Having fun for all to see.

Blue

Calm oceans and clear skies,
sun-lit lakes in the countryside.
Denim jeans and canvas shoes,
luxuriant silk pajamas.
Cobalt glass beads, a sapphire ring,
and a treasured antique necklace.
Spring irises, summer hydria,
and fragrant forget-me-nots.
Bubbly soda and tart candy,
sweet blueberry pie.
Sporty cars, a comfortable chair,
and that favorite cup for tea.
These things are best, especially when blue.

The Mind's Eye

The mind's eye sees more than we know.
The mind's eye dreams for a painter.
The mind's eye is the writer's window.
The mind's eye sees souls.
The mind's eye understands our pasts.
The mind's eye imagines our future.
The mind's eye knows our loves.
The mind's eye understands our hates.
The mind's eye is our soul's point of view.

Doodling

I scratch and doodle
Whatever entices my noodle.
A scribble,
Or even an ink dribble,
A castle in the sky,
Or a pink, puffy hi,
A cute, curly poodle,
Whatever; I always scratch and doodle.

Dragon Song

The song of dragons, I sing!
With that beast's power, it will ring!
Dragons of the sea and dragons of the sky above what we see!

Sing to the windblown song!
Sing to the wing beats!

A song for all colored scale, with dragon voices it yells!
Sing of lindworm and wyvern bazaar, for both dragons they are!

Sing to the windblown song!
Sing to the wing beats!

Dragons all with power are born!
Only dragons, for dragons will morn!
For in their veins runs blood of bile!
All dragons' breaths are vile!

Sing to the windblown song!
Sing to the wing beats!

For victims harm, you do; things of good will kill all of you!
Knight's blades spill dark blood!
You will pay for harming the good of heart's rights!

Sing to the windblown song!
Sing to the wing beats!

A dragon's power will be gone, when all that's left is a pile of bone!
A dragon is nothing but lore; there they will stay forever and more!

Sing to the windblown song.
Sing to the wing beats!
Sing to the dragon song!

Of Blue and Green

The sea of blue,
The ocean of green.
Both possess beauty,
In them calm serenity.
Beneath a surface of glass,
Swims a world of brilliant color.
Blue backdrops a landscape,
Trees of coral, and flowering creatures.
Green backdrops a ballet,
Fish of red, yellow, and white.
Spritely dolphins play,
While whales sing.
The seas and oceans are a symphony of blue and green.

Irises

Sea of wild green,
Violet and blue foam atop it.
Butterflies dip and dive,
Caressing beards of yellow.
Blue and violet foam are a feast
Upon a magic, green sea.

Little Tiger

Little tiger, little tiger,
Why are you so small?
Little tiger, little tiger,
I hear your little paws not at all.
Little tiger, little tiger,
You come treading down the hall.
Little tiger, little tiger,
I laugh when you pounce on your little ball.
Little tiger, little tiger,
You're my kitten, not even ankle tall.

The Ki'lin

Kirin or Ki'lin, what a creature?
What are you supposed to be?
Are you a dragon, lion, or unicorn?
Can you tell good from evil?
In your heart, or does your mind see?
Do you prance like a calf,
Or sit wisely under a persimmon tree?
Kirin or Ki'lin, you're a fantastic creature.
We might know what you're supposed to be.
You are a dragon, lion, and unicorn.
A perfect combination of all three.
You can tell good from evil.
Your heart and mind does see.
You prance like a calf,
And sit wisely under a persimmon tree.

My Cats

My cats have been many.
I wouldn't overlook any.
I once had a burly, gray tom;
He was a big guy and never hurried.
A red tabby, I became his mommy
Because he was orphaned and needed one.
One was a Halloween-black cat;
He was wonderful company.
I owned a tortoise shell that was short and fat;
She was a cat made of spit and vinegar.
Now I've got another.
So many cats who were my friends.
I will not forget each and every one
When I bring home a new kitten.
If I could, I'd give every cat my home,
Heartbroken when I see the homeless.

Too Much, Not Enough

Mankind has known fear,
Known it real and unreal to this very year.
Some fear fantasy born,
Then some real and hard as cow horn.
Fantasy poison of a wyvern wing,
Solid death from a hypodermic sting.
Fantastic fear from a troll army of a dark lord,
Real danger from a new type of man horde.
Phantom dragon claws piercing an armored head,
Painfully true fire pain of bullet lead.
Unicorn soft and supple, near us maybe,
True innocents in the new face of a baby.
A highland castle, clean, protected and peaceful;
Streets safely open and whole cities totally useful.
A fair fairy queen who is peace-loving but stern;
Plenty to go around, nothing to gain but only earn.
Mankind has known safety,
Known it real and unreal, until lately.
Some happiness fantasy spawn,
Some of it real and as faint as a yawn.
What's too much?
It there not enough?

Interplanetary Zoo

Apricot apes from the moon.
Blue boas spotted maroon.
Cerise cockatoos in a golden cage.
Dun donkeys very old of age.
Ebony emus tall enough to ride.
Florescent flamingos dancing with pride.
Green gorillas from mars.
Hazel horses behind lead bars.
Indigo ibexes with horns of stone.
Jade jackals gnawing on a bone.
Khaki kangaroos a hundred free high.
Lilac monkeys hanging from blue trees.
Neon nautiluses the size of fleas.
Orange octopuses that glow in the dark.
Pink penguins that can bark.
Quinine quails from far away Quars.
Red rabbits that like granola bars.
Silver seals from seas like glass.
Teal turtles with shells colored like grass.
Umber unicorns with eyes of rainbows.
Violet vixen wearing bright pink bows.
White walruses that have tusks of ivory.
Xanthis xenobats from far away Jenovory.
Yellow yaks with very wooly backs.
Zinc zebras whose stripes are many shades of blacks.

Dance Eternal

Round and round they swirl,
To an unheard song.
Each a nicely dressed lady.
One in red,
A dainty one, a billowy attire of multicolor.
Some with children,
Others with none.
One with a halo turned on its side,
And one with a delicate entourage.
Glitter-strewn is the ballroom,
Dance each to an unsung song.
The great, yellow, fiery conductor guiding,
They are all his ladies.
They dance eternal.

Technological Dinosaurs

Computers, computers everywhere!
But not a drop o' ink.
Where? Where am I to think?
A monitor here or a desktop there:
Papers and books are my mind's den.
So give me my paper and pen.
Yes, I give thanks to technological dinosaurs.
Computers may quickly go into fossilization.
Unplugged there isn't much for modernization.
Computers, computers everywhere,
Without their zap don't think.
So where? Where is some ink?

Candy

Oh, how people love candy.
Chocolate fudge,
Rich and thick.
Toffee or peanut brittle,
Crunchy and sticky.
Taffy and caramel,
Chewy and soft.
Candy cane and rock candy,
Sweet, minty, and long-lasting.
Oh, how people love candy.
But, alas, we go to the dentist!

Little Frog

Smooth glass green,
Eyes like big marbles:
A staring parody.
Long, spindly legs like springs,
His peep a sweet spring song.

Closet Door

What's behind my closet door
Really scares me to the core.
In there is another lore
Of goblins and their slimy gore.

At midnight they dance on my floor,
And my bed sheet edges they've torn.
At last when dancing is a bore,
They return to where my clothes I do store.

Dad laughs because I fear my closet door.
He opens it to show me they are no more.
I asked, "Where are the goblins and gore?
Why are they not in their closet lore?"

He smiled and said, "Far away on another shore,
Where they went to find gold ore."
Now at midnight they don't dance on my floor,
And now I do not fear that closet door.

Fair Unicorn

O, that fair unicorn o' mine,
How prettily does your lacquer and brass shine.
Around and around you chase,
With pretty colored animals you race.

Tigers and lions can keep pace,
Adorned with ribbons and lace.
Dance! Dance to a song with a simple rhyme,
Forever frozen life without time.

A bright child sees you, his steed,
One quick ride is all he'll need.
From wooden blocks you were born,
I chipped you free, down to your horn.

O, that fair unicorn o' mine,
Beautifully does your lacquer and brass shine.

Unicorn Pony

One day a girl rode her pony to the glade.
Where flowers of all colors bloom.
There many bouquets she made,
To return to her mother's room.
Her pony then ran, his black tail flying.
She stood to call and
Did not, for under a tree a pony was lying.
The strange, white pony stood,
To greet her shabby pet.
The white pony's forelock like a hood,
The two's noses met.
The white pony darted away,
But not too much.
He looked at her in a strange way,
A way that had a warm touch.
The white pony tossed its head,
To reveal beneath white hair a spark of gold.
She recalled stories of unicorns once read
By her mother that were old.
The white pony then walked into
The forest beyond slowly.
Then he was gone like morning dew.
She would remember this moment.

Park Unicorn

Springtime the birds came,
Both wild and tame.
They sat upon his stony self,
Like dolls on a shelf.

Summer came with toys,
Sailboats of little boys.
The children in his pool,
Under his horn, safe, stay cool.

Fall came with colors of fire,
A man to remove them they hire.
The man, he looked at him,
His gray self somehow dim.

Winter came, making him alone,
Because all were gone.
His pool became ice in his heart,
And he did burst apart.

Spring came again to find him gone,
Leaving other fountain animals alone.
When people came, the one with a horn,
They noticed not the gone Unicorn.

THE END